MY FLAVOUR OF WORDS

FROM INK TO EMOTION

KARIMULLA SHAIK

India | USA | UK

Copyright © KARIMULLA SHAIK
All Rights Reserved.

This book has been self-published with all reasonable efforts taken to make the material error-free by the author. No part of this book shall be used, reproduced in any manner whatsoever without written permission from the author, except in the case of brief quotations embodied in critical articles and reviews.

The Author of this book is solely responsible and liable for its content including but not limited to the views, representations, descriptions, statements, information, opinions, and references ["Content"]. The Content of this book shall not constitute or be construed or deemed to reflect the opinion or expression of the Publisher or Editor. Neither the Publisher nor Editor endorse or approve the Content of this book or guarantee the reliability, accuracy, or completeness of the Content published herein and do not make any representations or warranties of any kind, express or implied, including but not limited to the implied warranties of merchantability, fitness for a particular purpose.

The Publisher and Editor shall not be liable whatsoever...

Made with ❤ on the BookLeaf Publishing Platform
www.bookleafpub.in
www.bookleafpub.com

Dedication

To the ones who shaped my journey, i dedicate this book to my beloved family, whose unwavering support and love have been my greatest strength. To my friends, who nurtured my creativity with their encouragement. To every soul who finds solace in poetry and most importantly, to the divine presence guiding my path.

This book is a tribute to the experiences, emotions, and moments that define life. May these words resonate with those who seek meaning - My Flavour of Words.

Preface

poetry has always been my way of capturing emotions and reflections on life. Our Flavor of Words is a collection of poems that delve into various aspects of our journey education, failure, spirituality, and even historical pieces like The Farmer. Each poem carries a piece of my heart, written the hope that it touches yours.

This book is not about words; it is about the lessons they leave behind. Some moments uplift us, while who we are. through these pages, i invite you embark on a journey of introspection, nostalgia, and inspiration.

I hope this book finds a place in your heart and reminds you that no experience is ever truly lost, only woven into the flavour of our words

Acknowledgements

This book would not have been possible without the support, inspiration and encouragement of many individuals.

First and foremost, i am deeply grateful to my family, who have stood by me every step of the way, encouraging me to follow my passion. Your love and belief in me have my greatest motivation.

I extend my heartfelt thanks to my friends and well-wishers, who have supported my creative pursuits and offered valuable feedback. your encouragement has given me the confidence to share my words with the world.

I am thankful to my mentors and teachers, whose guidance has shaped my perspective on life and literature. your wisdom has played a crucial role in my growth as a writer.

Lastly, i express my sincere gratitude to every reader who picks up this book. Poetry is meant to be felt and if my words resonate with even one soul, i consider my purpose fulfilled.

1. BICYCLE

In childhood days, with winds so free,
My cycle was pure joy to me
Through schoolyard lanes and morning light,
It rode with me, my heart so light

So many tales it holds inside,
Some funny spins, some crazy rides.
With every turn and every fall,
It taught me life - it gave me all

A middle-class man's gentle plane,
Through sun and storm, through joy and pain.
To work, to home, to market near,
It rolled with hope, it rolled with cheer

With kids behind and bags held tight,
It carried dreams into the night.
A father's strength, a silent vow,
On two small wheels, he made it now

One pedal up, the other down,
Like smiles and tears that come around.
Life, too, goes in this gentle sway
We rise, we fall, and find our way

The bell that rings upon the street,
Is like God's hand, both kind and sweet.
It calls, it warns, it sings, it plays,
Like fate that guides our moving days

Sometimes two hearts ride side by side,
In love's sweet breeze, they gently glide.
With balance, care, and gentle pace,
Together they life's path embrace

So ride your life like you ride a bike
With steady hands through calm or strike.
Don't stop at bumps, just move ahead,
Let every fall lift you instead

For in this ride of gears and grace,
You'll find your truth, your rightful place.
A bicycle, though simple, shows
The way a balanced journey goes.

2. CHOOSE LIFE

CHOOSE LIFE

Suicide's not the way to go,
Though pain is real, let courage grow.
Storms will pass, the night will end,
Hold on tight, my dear young friend

Stress and struggle cloud your mind,
But brighter days, you soon will find.
Life is tough - but so are you,
There's nothing that you cannot do

Don't give up, don't say goodbye,
Spread your wings and choose to try.
From streets to seats of power and grace,
We all must run life's trying race

So breathe, believe, and stand up tall
Your life, your fight, is worth it all.

3. EXAMS

Exams - a small test of what we know,
Yet for some kids, the worries grow.
Some are tense, their minds not clear,
The thought of results brings silent fear

Others confused, not sure what to write,
Lost in pressure, day and night.
In schools and colleges, stress is high,
Marks and ranks - the reason why

They want toppers, they want fame,
But never ask - what's the child's name?
Not all can shine in the same light,
Each has a way, each has a right

Are children humans, or just machines?
Is success only what marks mean?
Daily they're fed with lessons and books,
But no one stops, no one looks

Health ignored, joy dismissed,
Real learning often missed.
Some parents point at others' scores,
Setting targets, raising wars

Why can't they see, why don't they feel,
The pressure's real, the pain is real.
Exams are not the end, just a way,
To test the knowledge of yesterday

A ticket to life? Maybe, not more
There's so much beyond a closed door.
School and college - just a part,
But not the measure of a child's heart

So let them breathe, let them grow,
Let their true potential show.
Exams are just a phase to face,
Not the end of the human race.

4. FRIENDSHIP

My friend, my soulmate, my mirror true,
Who corrects my faults with a heart so blue.
With words so kind and honesty pure,
His presence makes my troubles endure

So choose your friend with thoughtful care,
For friendship's rare, beyond compare.
It's honesty, it's loyal grace,
A baby's smile on a weary face

A friend is like the water clear,
In times of doubt, he draws me near.
When fear surrounds, he makes me brave,
A guiding light, a hand to save

Our bond is like the heart and blood,
In joy and pain, a constant flood.
At times, a brother - bold and wise,
At others, like a father's guise

My victories light up his face,
My worries slow his gentle pace.
No force can break what we both feel,
No crack can shake a bond so real.

For though we're two in flesh and bone,
In soul and mind - we are one alone.

5. FARMER

Many ask him, "Are you a farmer"
I've heard those words time and again
Yes! He is a farmer, standing proud,
With hands in soil, beneath the cloud

He knows the secrets of the land,
How food is born from his rough hands.
He feeds the people, one and all,
And lifts the nation's spirit tall

Farming's not just a simple word,
It's life's project - deep and heard.
Through fields and toil, day by day,
Some laborers earn their honest pay

Farming strengthens, like exercise,
It clears the mind, it makes us wise.
An art so rare, not all can claim,
Yet some embrace it, without fame

To some, it's business - crop and gold,
To others, stories deeply told.
It brings good income, sure and right,
With morning sun and stars at night

The farmer and farming not just two,
But twin flames of our nation's view.
Two eyes that help the country grow,
In sun, in rain, through high and low

We need the farmer - food and future,
They are our land's living sculpture.
Let's stand with them, give them their due,
For all they are, for all they do

The farmer is the King, we say,
Without a crown, yet leads the way.
No throne, no robe, no palace door
Yet feeds a nation, rich and poor.

6. FLOWERS

I am not just a flower
I bloom with many names in Nature's garden.
To some, I am Jasmine,
To others, a Lotus,
To a few, I'm known as Rose.
Each name, a new identity,
Each face, a new fragrance in the breeze

I play my part in every season,
On every occasion, I hold meaning.
At a girl's coming of age, I rest gently in her hair.
At a wedding, I touch two hearts with silent care.
In moments of triumph, I am held high with pride
In the hands of joy, I do not hide

But my role is never the same
With each moment, my purpose will change.
I do not long to live forever on a tree,
Nor to sit in silence before the deity.
I do not wish to stand
Between a husband and a wife, hand in hand

Sometimes, I am the symbol of love,
Soft and sweet, sent from above.

Sometimes, I carry the scent of memory,
A token in hands during victory or ceremony.
And sometimes, I line the path of those who've passed
A quiet farewell, a bloom that doesn't last

But if I could choose my destiny,
Let me bloom in a soldier's victory.
Let me fall not in sorrow, but in pride
A final salute for those who died.

7. FREEDOM

Freedom a mighty word,
not easily given,
not gently taken

It is not a gift,
but a fight,
a flame seized
from clenched fists
for a greater cause

For this word,
so many have fallen not for themselves,
but for the children,
for the future,
for a community yet to bloom

In school, when a child stumbles or strays, a parent cries,
"You're taking my child's freedom!"

In labor, the owner stands tall but beneath his feet,
the worker's freedom is buried.

In politics, a leader claims the voice,
but the people lose their own.

In government halls,
only the voter holds the final key
but even that is too often taken.

Freedom, no one gives it freely.
No handout.
No easy offering.

We must rise, reach out,
grasp it with our own hands.

Now even in homes,
husband and wife argue not for love,
but for space, for breath,
for their own piece of sky.

They no longer seek
a long,
shared life only the freedom
to walk alone.

Across the world,
generations battled, bled, died
for their country's name to fly free in the wind.

And yet, in any season,

any place - freedom does not come gently.

Only after storms, after pain,
after standing firm
through the hardest nights only then
does freedom come near...
and kiss us softly.

8. GOOGLE

For children I am an educational Bank

Students ask sports questions and answers

Un-employees check job information for their families

A traveler searches for journey details with me

A businessman finds his business expansion data

Some people do jobs in my company

For few persons I am home for their future

I am their strength for top class celebrities in the society

I am on the social media platform for politicians

I give equal priority in entire life for the poor and rich

Many people have many questions - different people different options

Where ever and whatever I am with the people

Because I am Google..!

9. JESUS

Oh my God

Can you hear me
once listen to me
once talk to me
once focus on me
I am your beloved person

Oh my God

Now I am inside of the problems of ocean
you are not caring me
Where are you now my dear
once can you see me
I thought I was your child

Oh God once bless me
oh god once save me
oh god once message me

Oh my God

My trust only you
my hope is only you

my strength is only you

Oh my God

Please accept my plea
I will rectify my mistakes
I live in your direction

Please,
give your blessings abundantly on me

Oh my God - oh my God..!

10. MY VILLAGE

When I remember my village, I feel so much joy,
A place of pure love, since I was a boy.
The people there, with hearts so true,
Live close to nature, in all that they do

They show their love in a gentle way,
With kind, soft words, they brighten the day.
They never shy from working hard,
Yet wear humility like a sacred guard

They know no ego, no pride or pretense,
Their kindness and care are deep and intense.
They farm the land with hands of grace,
And cherish their roots, their culture, their place

Family values guide their way,
In every word they choose to say.
They live to share, to give, to care,
Spreading joy everywhere

My first love bloomed on that sacred ground,
Where peace and purpose always surround
My village is my soul, my start,
The living rhythm of my heart

It's my emotion, my breath, my economy,
A timeless bond, a sweet symphony
Fresher than any freshener's scent,
Is the breeze from where my childhood went.

11. MY FRIEND

I have a friend, so true and kind,
A schoolmate once, now soul aligned
A roommate, teammate - side by side,
Through every storm and rising tide

He lifts me up, my energy spark,
A light that shines when days are dark.
He is my shadow, close and near,
With him around, I lose all fear

When I meet him, thoughts grow clear,
When I speak, the truth draws near
In times of trouble, he's the key,
The only one who sets me free

Our bond is pure, like skies so blue,
Like nature - clean, so fresh, so true.
In my life's path, he's rare to find,
A gem so precious, one of a kind

So handle with care, for none compare,
No one like him, now or elsewhere
His love is simple, calm and deep,
Humble, loyal - a bond we keep.

12. MEDICINE

Medicine - a path to heal,
A cure for wounds that time can't seal
For every pain, a different way,
A different role it comes to play

For bodies weak, it's pills and rest,
A doctor's touch, their very best
But not all pain is of the skin,
Some lie quietly deep within

A teacher's words, both kind and wise,
Can lift a student to the skies
A mother's hug, her silent prayer,
Can soothe a child's deepest despair

A coach's shout, a guiding hand,
Can help the player rise and stand
For every soul that's lost or torn,
A special cure is gently born

Not all will take the same relief,
For every heart holds different grief
A laborer, with daylong strife,
Finds peace in drink to soften life

In family bonds, where tensions rise,
Loyalty is the sweetest prize
In love, it's truth that soothes the pain,
A genuine heart - the healing rain

In politics, when lies run deep,
Truth wakes the voter from their sleep
In every role, in every place,
Medicine wears a different face

Sometimes it's words that touch the soul,
Or honesty that makes us whole
At times it's presence, pure and near,
A silent hug, a listening ear

So let us learn, and understand,
That healing takes a different hand
For every wound, both big and small,
There is a cure - one made for all.

13. NIGHT

Night falls-darkness wraps the world so tight,
A time of silence, rest, and quiet light
Not just the moon to gaze above,
But a world of truths, both harsh and love

Some find peace beneath its shade,
Some in night-shift jobs are made
Others read as hours drift,
While thoughts and dreams begin to lift

For some, it's lonely, cold, and deep,
For others, joy they get to keep
A moment shared with stars above,
Or talking soft to those they love

A middle-class man counts tomorrow's fate,
While the rich chase numbers late
The poor, they cherish family near
Their laughter soft, their minds sincere

Creators dream and bring to life
Their art, their words, their silent strife

The honest sleep with hearts at peace,
The crooked fear the night won't cease

In nighttime's hush, we face our soul,
See others' truths, both dark and whole
For masks slip off as silence grows,
And secret lives the night wind knows.

Currency, character - shifting hands,
In whispered deals or quiet plans
Oh, night! You're more than just the dark
You hold the world's most telling spark.

14. PROSTITUTE

Prostitution is old days its golden days
Prostitution in old days very important for society
Prostitution in old days good recognition from kings
When days are changed they are also change
Now a days prostitution is a one of the jobs
They are getting hi profile life status
Today their income sources are rich
They behave like a sales girl for herself
She can sale her beauty for unknown person
She can behave like clients wife
She can act like someone's love
She can engage men's life so much physical happiness
She is the Barbie-doll of broken heart boys
She is the queen of sex land
She can play many characters in her routine life
We can call her lighting lamp of night life
Prostitutes job life, she doesn't have chance to say no
No one wants to welcome prostitution in women's life
It depends upon their families,
her behavior and destiny made her prostitute
We can say she is the medicine of our society
Finally,
How to utilize medicine or prostitute
it depends upon men's attitude..!

15. SORRY to SAREE

Saree - the soul of Indian grace,
A timeless drape, a proud embrace
From freedom's fight to wedding nights,
It held our stories, dreams, and rights

Once, it flowed in every street,
Wrapped in pride, so calm, so sweet.
Mothers wore it, daughters too,
A thread of culture running through

But now I ask - how many wear,
This six-yard song with love and care?
Some now scoff, "Why should I try?"
"I'm modern now, not village-tied."

"Who are you to ask my way?"
"I wear what fits my mood today."
Yes, India's free, we choose our style,
But have we lost what made us smile?

A woman holds traditions dear,
Passed down with love, year by year
In saree, you're a symbol still,
Of strength, of grace, of iron will

It guards your form, it speaks your soul,
It plays a nurturing, vital role
From feeding babes with gentle hand,
To solving things we barely understand.

From past to now, the times have turned,
But saree's worth is yet unlearned
Less and less, it now appears,
Washed away by modern years.

Today's young hearts say "Sorry, Saree,"
Chasing trends, fast and airy
But remember those who wore it proud,
And made our nation stand unbowed.

Let's not forget this woven art,
That beats with India's beating heart
Save the saree, let it shine
A gift to pass through time's long line.

16. SPORTS

Sports will teach us how to live,
To rise, to strive, to learn, to give
With every game, a lesson springs,
Sports will give us successful wings

In fields where dreams and sweat collide,
Leadership is born with pride
Punctuality, grace, and mental might,
Sports guide us to what is right

They shape our bodies, strong and fit,
Fueling fire, refusing to quit
A sporting win, a shining name,
Can bring us joy, respect, and fame

Teamwork blooms in every play,
Learning to lead in a humble way
A sportsperson, calm and true,
Is simple in heart, in actions too

Sometimes royal, sometimes raw,
The path of sports holds us in awe
A career, a calling, a lifelong flame,
For some, it's the truest aim

It builds the spirit, brave and bright,
To face each challenge, day or night
With deep and strong values,
Sports help us all belong

Let's break it down, a name so grand
S for Sportiveness, where we stand
P for Positiveness, bold and free,
O for Oxygen, the breath to be
R for Right thinking, always wise,
T for the Test of behaviour that never lies
S for Sacrifice, pure and true
These are the values sports give you

So, stand up strong and play your part,
With a fearless soul and a lion's heart
A successful sportsperson knows the way
To face life's battles, come what may.

17. THE MARRIAGE RING

What magic lies in this marriage ring?
A golden band - a sacred thing
When first I wore it, joy was mine,
A symbol pure, a love divine

But days go by, and hearts may sway,
The glow it had begins to gray
This ring now feels a heavy load,
A path of love, a steep, steep road

So many feelings held inside,
So many tears we've tried to hide
At times I ask, am I still fit,
To wear this ring, or should I quit?

Once a promise, now a show
Just a mark of wealth to glow
Once a vow, now just a sale,
A love that's bought is bound to fail

Now it's business, now it's pride,
A token worn, yet hearts divide

Permission given, not through grace,
But just a ring - and not embrace

The bride, the groom, do they still see
The weight of love, the loyalty?
So quick to wear, so quick to lose,
A bond so sacred, yet they choose

Dear young hearts, don't treat it light,
Be true in love, hold each other tight
This ring's not gold, it's something more
A bridge between two hearts, two shores

It joins two lives, two souls, two kin,
A future waiting to begin
So, wear it not just on your hand,
But in your heart - where vows must stand.

18. TAEKWONDO

Taekwondo means it's a martial art

Taekwondo is a life of peace

Taekwondo indicates its self discipline

Taekwondo is a fight of life

Taekwondo is a desire for character

Taekwondo is a moral culture

Taekwondo signifies it's a courage

Taekwondo sets out a philosophy

Taekwondo aims one punch

Taekwondo stands for one world

Taekwondo is the new way to learn

Taekwondo is for "Every one"

19. TIME

When time is with us, we often fail to see its worth,
We take it for granted, not knowing its true birth

But when we face struggles, our countdown begins,
And time starts shaping our losses and wins

Through good days or bad, it quietly flows,
Guiding our journey, as only time knows

So cherish each moment you have to yourself,
For time, once lost, is a vanished wealth

When we value time, it returns the grace,
Rewarding our efforts at every pace

So don't waste your time, my dear friends,
Use it wisely before it ends

We can buy a watch - but not the time,
Each second gone is a silent chime

The wall clock reminds us how to live each day,
Keeping us steady on our routine way

Time will reveal who stands by your side,
Exposing true faces others might hide

Time doesn't change people
it simply unveils,
The truth beneath all the masks and tales

Time is money, yet more than gold
It's a treasure that can't be bought or sold.

20. WRITER

They say you're a creator, a weaver of tales,
You build whole worlds where truth prevails
From stories deep to characters bold,
In your ink, a thousand lives unfold

You craft the lines, the taglines sing,
You make mere words take flight on wing
Your vision sharp, future in sight,
Guiding generations through the night

A song, a script, a fiery speech,
No realm of thought beyond your reach
You hold a mirror to the age,
And etch rebellion on the page

You carry hearts - their joy, their ache,
The silent tears, the smiles they fake
A voice for those who cannot shout,
You write what others dare not out

For you, imagination has no fence,
A boundless sky of rare suspense
No one can touch the heights you climb,
Or bend the rhythm of your rhyme

You hold the soul of all that's felt
In every word, emotions melt
So now, today, society sees
The writer holds the master keys

A SIM card plugged into the age,
Recharged with truth on every page
We speak to him, we trust him whole,
He writes and heals - the common soul.

21. YOGA

Yoga is not just a word
It is everything to us.

Sometimes, yoga is our exercise,
At times, it heals like a doctor
Sometimes, it works like medicine,
A soothing balm for body and soul

Yoga brings peaceful, restful sleep,
And lifts our minds with quiet strength
It gives us fresh and hopeful thoughts,
A clearer view of days to come.

At times, yoga is our well-wisher,
Guiding us through joy and strife
It builds a bond with Mother Nature,
And strengthens ties with human life

Yoga is the true life line
A path to live long, healthy days
A sacred map to reach the divine,
To speak with God in silent ways

So, Yoga for everything - everything in Yoga
Yoga for all - all for Yoga.

www.ingramcontent.com/pod-product-compliance
Lightning Source LLC
Chambersburg PA
CBHW070040070426
42449CB00012BA/3117